W9-BCT-074

Covered in Water

by Ellen Lawrence

Consultant:

Howard Perlman, Hydrologist

BEARPORT
PUBLISHING

New York, New York

Credits

Cover, © Lkunl/Shutterstock; 4, © NASA; 5, © Lissandra Melo/Shutterstock; 6, © Matej Kastelic/Shutterstock; 7, © Ashley Whitworth/Shutterstock; 8, © Vlad6I/Shutterstock; 9L, © vovan/Shutterstock; 9C, © parafox/Shutterstock; 9R, © Elena Arkadova/Shutterstock; 10, © Ruby Tuesday Books; 11, © Flip Nicklin/Minden Pictures/FLPA; 11B, © D. P. Wilson/FLPA; 12T, © Ekaterina Pokrovsky/Shutterstock; 12B, © huyangshu/Shutterstock; 13, © Johnny Lye/Shutterstock; 14T, © Oleg Gekman/Shutterstock; 14B, © Jerry Sanchez/Shutterstock; 15T, © Cosmographics; 15, © SeaWiFS Project, NASA/Goddard Space Flight Center and ORBIMAGE; 16T, meunierd/Shutterstock; 16B, © NASA; 17, © Robert Harding Picture Library Ltd/Alamy; 18T, © patpitchaya/Shutterstock; 18B, © gnatuk/Shutterstock; 19, © Shutterstock; 20T, © Sundraw Photography/Shutterstock; 20B, © Sharon Day/Shutterstock; 21, © Juergen Wackenhut/Shutterstock; 22T, © M. Unal Ozmen/Shutterstock; 22C, © Gyorgy Barna/Shutterstock; 22B, © Digital Media Pro/Shutterstock; 23TL, © Ulkastudio/Shutterstock; 23TC, © Tatiana Popova/Shutterstock; 23TR, © Mocha VP/Shutterstock; 23BL, © Northphoto/Shutterstock; 23BC, © Yuriy Kulik/Shutterstock; 23BR, © Lskywalker/Shutterstock.

Publisher: Kenn Goin
Senior Editor: Joyce Tavolacci
Creative Director: Spencer Brinker
Design: Emma Randall
Photo Researcher: Ruby Tuesday Books Ltd

Library of Congress Cataloging-in-Publication Data

Names: Lawrence, Ellen, 1967– author.
Title: Covered in water / by Ellen Lawrence.
Description: New York, New York : Bearport Publishing, [2016] | Series: Drip, drip, drop: Earth's water | Audience: Ages 5–9.
    | Includes bibliographical references and index.
Identifiers: LCCN 2015037721| ISBN 9781943553266 (library binding) | ISBN 1943553262 (library binding)
Subjects: LCSH: Hydrology—Juvenile literature. | Hydrologic cycle—Juvenile literature. | Water—Juvenile literature.
Classification: LCC GB662.3 .L39 2016 | DDC 551.48—dc23
LC record available at http://lccn.loc.gov/2015037721

For more information, write to Bearport Publishing Company, Inc., 45 West 21st Street, Suite 3B, New York, New York 10010. Printed in the United States of America.

10 9 8 7 6 5 4 3 2 1

Contents

Our Watery World

From puddles and ponds to lakes and oceans—there's a lot of water on Earth!

That's because about 70 percent of Earth's surface is covered in water.

So where is water found on Earth, and is it all the same?

Let's find out by exploring our watery world.

Earth from space

Atlantic Ocean

Pacific Ocean

Earth is often called the Blue Planet. Why? It looks mostly blue from space.

4

Niagara Falls

In a notebook, make a list of all the places you've seen water in your neighborhood in the past week.

Salty or Fresh?

There are two types of water on Earth—salt water and fresh water.

Salt water is found in oceans and seas, and in some lakes.

It contains many tiny salt **particles**, which give it a salty taste.

Fresh water also contains some salt, but not enough to make it taste salty.

This type of water is found in ponds, streams, rivers, and in many lakes.

a freshwater lake

The salt in salt water comes from rocks on land that contain particles of salt. When waves break off bits of rocky cliffs, they carry the rocks and salt particles into the water.

Do you think most of Earth's water is salty or fresh?

rocky cliffs

salty ocean water

Earth's Water

About 97 percent of the water on Earth is salt water.

The rest of Earth's water is fresh water.

Some of the fresh water is liquid.

However, most of Earth's fresh water is frozen solid.

It's found as ice and snow in very cold parts of the world, such as the Arctic.

salt water

Earth's Water

liquid salt water

liquid fresh water

ice, or frozen fresh water

liquid fresh water

ice and snow in the Arctic

Some of Earth's water is actually underground. When rain falls and snow melts, water soaks deep into the soil. This water is known as groundwater.

rain

groundwater

Oceans and Seas

Earth has five vast oceans and many smaller seas.

They are home to hundreds of thousands of different kinds of animals and plants.

Some tiny ocean creatures called zooplankton are smaller than the period at the end of this sentence.

Others, such as whales, are among the largest animals on Earth.

Some parts of the ocean are extremely deep. The deepest known place is in the Pacific Ocean. It's called Challenger Deep and is nearly 7 miles (11.2 km) below the water's surface.

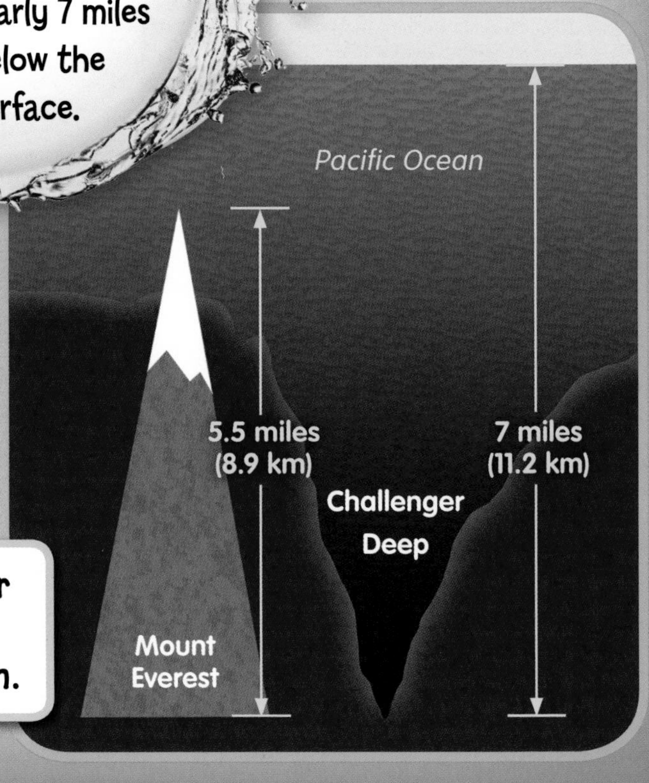

Pacific Ocean

5.5 miles (8.9 km)

7 miles (11.2 km)

Challenger Deep

Mount Everest

This diagram shows the depth of Challenger Deep compared to the height of Mount Everest, which is the tallest mountain on Earth.

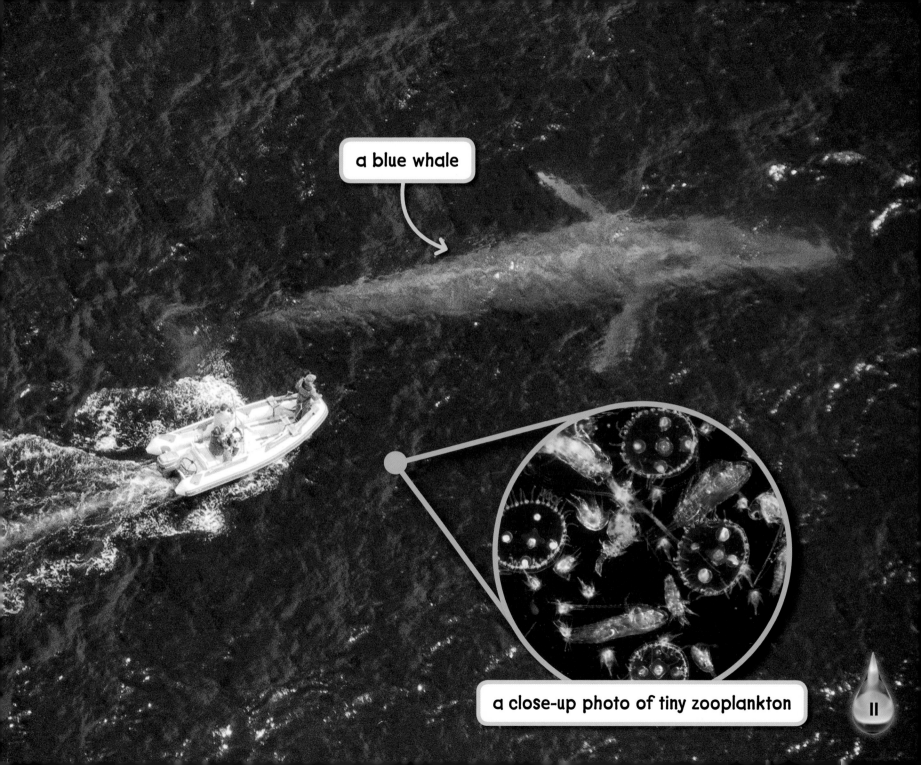

Rushing Rivers

Many rivers crisscross the planet, but how do they form?

When rain falls and snow melts, water trickles across the land.

The flowing water forms small streams that join together to make a river.

As the river rushes over the land, more streams flow into it and it grows wider.

Finally, the river flows into a lake, a sea, or an ocean.

rainwater

stream

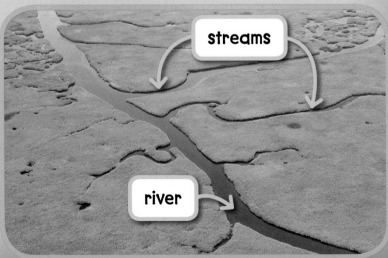

streams

river

mouth of river

ocean

river

The bottom of a river is called a riverbed. The sides of a river are called banks. The place where a river joins the ocean is known as a mouth.

13

Lakes and Ponds

A lake is a large, deep body of water that's surrounded by land.

The deepest lake in the world is Lake Baikal in Russia.

Lakes get water from streams and rivers that flow into them.

A pond is a small, still body of water that may be just a few feet deep.

Most ponds form when a hollow part of the ground fills with rainwater.

Lake Baikal is
1 mile (1.6 km) deep.

a pond

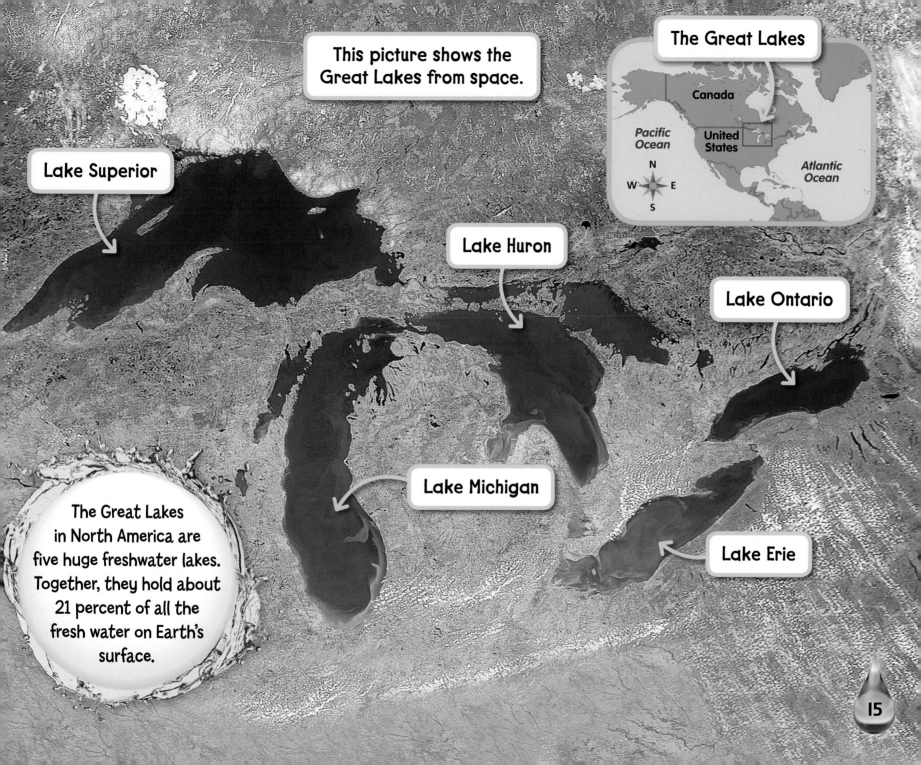

This picture shows the Great Lakes from space.

The Great Lakes

Canada

Pacific Ocean

United States

Atlantic Ocean

N W E S

Lake Superior

Lake Huron

Lake Ontario

Lake Michigan

Lake Erie

The Great Lakes in North America are five huge freshwater lakes. Together, they hold about 21 percent of all the fresh water on Earth's surface.

Frozen Water

Much of Earth's fresh water is solid ice and snow.

This frozen water is found in ice sheets, **glaciers**, icebergs, and on snowy mountaintops.

Ice sheets are huge areas of ice that stretch across cold parts of the world.

Antarctica is covered by an ice sheet that's larger than the United States!

Not all Earth's water is on the planet's surface. Where else do you think some of the water might be?

An iceberg is a huge chunk of floating ice.

Pacific Ocean

South America

Southern Ocean

ice sheet

Antarctica

glacier

A glacier is a thick mass of ice and snow that covers a large area of land. Glaciers move very slowly, like giant, frozen rivers. Some glaciers move just a few feet each year.

The Water Cycle

Some of Earth's water is stored in the sky as clouds.

When water on Earth is warmed by the Sun, some of it changes into a **gas** called **water vapor**.

Then it floats high into the sky.

Cold air turns the vapor back into droplets of liquid water that form clouds.

Then the water in the clouds falls back down to Earth as rain in a process called the **water cycle**.

rain

Sometimes, water vapor gets so cold that it freezes and becomes ice. The tiny bits of ice stick together to form snowflakes. Then they fall down to Earth as snow.

The Water Cycle in Action

The water droplets form clouds.

The water vapor cools and becomes water droplets.

Water vapor rises into the sky.

Rain or snow falls from the clouds.

lake

pond

19

Water in Our World

What makes our beautiful blue planet so special?

It's covered in water.

All living things—including people, animals, and plants—need water to survive.

Without water, Earth would be a lifeless place.

There would be no forests, no fields, no animals—and no you!

People collect fresh water in large lakes called **reservoirs**. This water is used for drinking, cooking, and washing. It's carried from reservoirs through miles of pipes to people's homes.

a reservoir

Science Lab

There's lots of water on Earth but only a small amount is liquid fresh water. That's why it's important to use water wisely.

Have Clean Teeth—and Save Water!

One way to save water is to turn off the faucet when you brush your teeth. How much water will this save? Let's investigate!

You will need a measuring cup.

1. Hold a measuring cup under the faucet. Turn on the water and then count how many seconds it takes to collect a pint (0.5 l) of water. For example, it might take five seconds.

2. Next, brush your teeth with the water running, and count how many seconds this takes. For example, it might take 60 seconds.

   So how many pints of water can be collected in 60 seconds?

   If a pint (0.5 l) comes out of the faucet in 5 seconds, just divide 60 seconds by 5 to find out how much water was used.

   $$60 \div 5 = 12$$

   The answer is 12 pints (5.7 l) of water.

   If you turn off the faucet when you brush your teeth, you could save 12 pints (5.7 l) of water!

Science Words

gas (GASS) matter that floats in air and is neither a liquid nor a solid; most gases, such as water vapor, are invisible

glaciers (GLAY-shurz) huge, slow-moving, river-like masses of ice

particles (PAR-ti-kuhlz) tiny pieces of something

reservoirs (REZ-ur-vwarz) natural or humanmade lakes where people store water

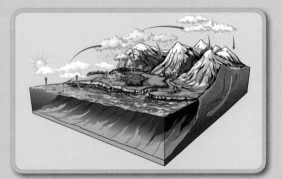

water cycle (WAH-tur SYE-kuhl) the movement of water from Earth up into the sky to form clouds, and then back down to Earth again

water vapor (WAH-tur VAY-pur) water that has changed into a gas; water vapor rises and spreads out through the air

Index

Read More

Lawrence, Ellen. *Poisoned Rivers and Lakes (Green World, Clean World)*. New York: Bearport (2014).

Spilsbury, Louise. *What are Rivers, Lakes, and Oceans? (Let's Find Out! Earth Science)*. New York: Rosen (2014).

Yu, Da-jeong. *The Flow of Water*. Minneapolis, MN: Lerner (2015).

Learn More Online

To learn more about Earth's water, visit
www.bearportpublishing.com/DripDripDrop

About the Author

Ellen Lawrence lives in the United Kingdom. Her favorite books to write are those about nature and animals. In fact, the first book Ellen bought for herself, when she was six years old, was the story of a gorilla named Patty Cake that was born in New York's Central Park Zoo.